MOO MOO

Written and Illustrated by
Lois Simon

Published by
High Pitched Hum Publishing

www.highpitchedhum.net

HIGH PITCHED HUM and the mosquito are trademarks of High Pitched
Hum Publishing.

ISBN: 978-0-9885818-8-3
Copyright © 2015 by Lois Simon
Copyright © 2015 art by Lois Simon

For

Billy
Beth
and
Stuart

Moo Moo was an ordinary cow in all respects but one. She had an unusually strong craving for cherry lollypops.

MOᴼᴼᴼ MOᴼᴼᴼ

While all the other cows were content to lie in the fields swishing the flies off their backs and eating grass, Moo Moo would spend hours licking cherry lollypops.

In fact, she had a special place to store her supply. It was under the haystack to the right of the barn. She would sit there all day licking her lollypops and dreaming of lollypop trees.

Everyone for miles around knew when Moo Moo was licking cherry lollypops. She would cry in a loud happy voice...

MOᵒᵒᵒ MOᵒᵒᵒ

And everyone for miles around knew when Moo Moo was not licking cherry lollypops. She would cry in a loud mournful voice...

Moooo Moooo

One day, something happened that had never happened before. Everyone who lived around the countryside was aware of the problem. Moo Moo went to the haystack to the right of the barn, and searched for cherry lollypops. There were none to be found.

She had eaten her entire supply, and let out the most mournful

MOOOOMOOOO's

her neighbors had ever heard.

Immediately Moo Moo began to search for cherry lollypops, and what a search it turned out to be.

She swam rivers and lakes,

climbed the tallest mountains,

and searched the darkest forests.

The great desert of Arabia was searched...

The jungles of Africa were searched...

The streets of China were searched...

The tulip fields of Holland were searched...

And the snow fields of Alaska were searched.

Around the world she traveled searching for cherry lollypops. Her mournful cry was heard by all...

MOooo MOooo

Finally, a very sad, Moo Moo returned home with not one cherry lollypop.

She went to the haystack to the right of the barn and cried in the loudest most mournful voice yet...

MOooo MOooo

Suddenly, a little bird flying high overhead stopped to see why Moo Moo was crying. Moo Moo between moos, told her story.

When Moo Moo told her story, the little bird threw back her head and laughed loudly.

"Oh Moo Moo, you silly cow" she chirped, "to travel so far when what you want is right here and has been all the time. If you had stopped to look and think instead of running off to far away places, you would have seen the new candy store four haystacks, two barns and three apple trees down on the right." "Candy store," said Moo Moo with the first hint of a smile on her face in months.

With that, she ran past the

    four haystacks

    two barns and

    three apple trees,

and there on the right was a brightly colored,
filled to the brim, candy store.

Moo Moo opened the door and there on the counter were jars and jars of brightly colored lollypops, and many were cherry, in all shapes and sizes.

If you could have seen Moo Moo's face! She was so excited she had to sit down and rest for a few minutes.

When she recovered, Moo Moo picked out the largest cherry lollypop in the store, and do you know what she said when she licked it?

MOᵒᵒᵒ MOᵒᵒᵒ